ELIZABETH
GOLDEN JUBILEE

ELIZABETH
GOLDEN JUBILEE

A. E. GAUNTLETT

p

This is a Parragon Book
First published in 2002

Parragon
Queen Street House
4 Queen Street
Bath, BA1 1HE, UK

Text ©Parragon
Photographs copyright page 96

Produced by Atlantic Publishing

Origination by Croxsons PrePress

A catalogue record for this book is available from
the British Library.
ISBN 0-75257-908-8

Acknowledgements

Thanks to
Christine Hoy, Cliff Salter,
Richard Betts, Peter Wright,
Trevor Bunting, Simon Taylor,
Stephen Atkinson, Steve Torrington,
Dave Sheppard, Brian Jackson,
Alan Pinnock, Paul Rossiter John Dunne,
Ian and Alice Gauntlett.

Printed in China

Introduction

Happy and glorious

The year 2002 marks the Golden Jubilee of Queen Elizabeth II, the most popular and successful monarch in British history. She came to the throne at a time when the country was still trying to shrug off the influence of World War II and has taken it forward into a period of enormous change and diversity. As sovereign, her responsibilities are daunting but the commitment and dedication she has given to these duties has never wavered since the day she became Queen.

She is an enigmatic lady. She has a public face and a personal side that the majority of the nation never sees. Her life is dictated by a long list of public appearances and annual events that she attends tirelessly and with enormous enthusiasm. People who know her talk of a dedicated mother, a loyal wife and a woman with a wicked sense of humour! Passionate about horses, she is one of the most knowledgeable breeders of racehorses in the country. She is also a keen photographer and has passed these interests onto her children. Annual holidays are taken in the same locations at the same time every year but she treasures these occasions when she can disappear from the public eye and truly relax.

Now in the year of the Golden Jubilee, the Queen has continued to take a lead and has been instrumental in planning the celebrations around the country and around the world. She remains determined to meet as many people as possible, breaking away from as much formality as security will allow. It is a year of great celebration and the Queen will use every opportunity to enjoy it!

ELIZABETH

GOLDEN JUBILEE

Born on 21st April 1926, the Duke and Duchess of York's eldest child Elizabeth was not originally destined to become Queen. In December 1936, her uncle, King Edward VIII chose to abdicate to marry Wallis Simpson, an American divorcee, less than a year after he had acceded to the throne. Suddenly, his brother, the shy Prince Albert, was thrust into the role of King and Elizabeth became heir to the throne. No longer were the family to lead the life of relatively minor royals, it was now their task to lead the country and take it through very difficult times ahead.

Elizabeth's father was crowned George VI. He led the country through the Second World War and its aftermath becoming a very popular and well-loved King. However, his health began to fail and in 1951 he had a lung removed. He died in his sleep at Sandringham on 6th February 1952 at the age of fifty six. Princess Elizabeth was in Kenya on tour with her husband, the Duke of Edinburgh at the time. They immediately flew back to Heathrow and were greeted in the early morning by the Prime Minister, Winston Churchill.

Elizabeth was only twenty-five when her father died, a naval wife and the mother of two very young children. From that day, the family's life changed dramatically. Suddenly they were thrust into the public eye – she had to cope with her responsibilities as a wife and mother, her own personal grief at losing a much-loved father and her duties as a sovereign.

The Queen has continued to build on her father's popularity. On her accession to the throne she was intent on going out to the nation to meet people, to talk to them, to understand their daily lives. Her own life is actually fixed by a rigid calendar of events. She attends the same functions from year to year and holidays are taken at fixed venues and dates. It is her Royal tours and visits that provide her with some variety - but she is always a public figure and face. For this reason, her holidays and the opportunities to follow her favourite sport – horse racing, are sacrosanct. Here she can be a private person, following her own interests and spending time with her family.

After she acceded the throne, the first major event was the Coronation on 6th June 1953. It was a glittering occasion and the young, beautiful Queen symbolised the country's optimism for the future. The country had taken a long time to shake off the effects of the war but at last, shortages and hardships were easing off and everyone was looking forward.

She spent much of the fifties visiting the Commonwealth countries and the colonies, establishing herself as the new monarch. This meant long periods of separation from her two children Charles and Anne. They spent most of this time with their grandmother, the Queen Mother and joined their parents for holidays whenever possible.

The beginning of the sixties was a very happy time for the family. Prince Andrew and Prince Edward were born and Princess Margaret married Anthony Armstrong-Jones. The Queen has always prioritised the times she has spent with her family and after the birth of Edward, she restricted her duties for a while. During this decade, the image of the monarchy was beginning to change and the Queen was instrumental in leading the way. It was she who

had insisted that the Coronation and the Christmas speeches were televised. She began the practice of holding informal lunches where she could establish contact with people from different walks of life and ended the long tradition of her own children having to bow and curtsey to her. She was determined to maintain as ordinary a family life as possible for her children and wanted them kept out of the limelight. She would allow photographs to be taken on specific occasions to satisfy the press.

In the seventies, the Queen wanted the image of the family to be presented more informally asking photographers to take portraits that were more relaxed in style. It was a decade of celebrations beginning with the Queen and the Duke of Edinburgh's Silver Wedding Anniversary. This was swiftly followed by Princess Anne's wedding and the Silver Jubilee. However, it ended in tragedy after the assassination of Lord Louis Mountbatten. He had a huge influence on the family and the shock remained with them for many years afterwards.

The eighties saw the Queen continuing to tour the world. With the Duke of Edinburgh, she toured widely including visits to the South Pacific, the Caribbean, the United States and Canada, Africa and India. The first half of the decade was dominated by the Falklands War and as the country's sovereign she also had the strain of knowing Prince Andrew was involved in combat. Family celebrations continued. The marriage of Prince Charles to Lady Diana Spencer took place in 1981 with enormous pageantry and spectacle. Four more grandchildren were born and Prince Andrew also married.

In 1990, the Queen Mother celebrated her ninetieth birthday and many birthday tributes were planned. The following year the Queen reached her sixty-fifth birthday without any intention of retiring. After the celebrations she immediately set off for an official tour of the States, closely followed by visits to Africa later in the year. Prince Philip also celebrated his seventieth birthday. Neither of them showed any sign of cutting back on their official engagements. She continued with her famous 'walkabouts' deriving much pleasure from meeting the waiting crowds. The decade was overshadowed by the death of Princess Diana in a car crash in Paris in 1997. By now separated from Prince Charles, her death sent shock waves around the world as thousands of mourners flocked to Kensington Palace to pay their respects. Her youngest son Edward married Sophie Rhys-Jones in 1999, ending the decade on a happier note.

The death of her beloved sister, Princess Margaret, in February of this year has cast a shadow over both the personal and public celebrations of the Queen's Golden Jubilee. But, the Queen is still working as hard as ever, determined to keep the pledge she made to her people – the commitment and pleasure she gets from this role is ever present.

Formal engagements

Elizabeth accompanies her family as George VI plants the first tree of the Commemorative Oak Tree Grove in Windsor Great Park. In June 1937, Elizabeth was already aware that one day she would wear the crown and the Palace was intent on preparing her carefully for this role. At the age of eleven she was becoming involved in formal functions with her parents and younger sister Margaret.

Opposite: July 1940 and Elizabeth and Margaret are given a motor launch trip on the Thames.

Frontispiece: Princess Elizabeth with her parents. She was born at 17 Bruton St, London W1 on the 21st April, 1926, was christened on the 29th May, 1926 in the Private Chapel at Buckingham Palace and was confirmed on the 28th March, 1942 in the Private Chapel at Windsor Castle.

First broadcast

Elizabeth made her first broadcast in 1940. It was a task that her father hated, due to a stammer, so the BBC used to record his voice in small sections at a time. Elizabeth, however, embraced the challenge and would record her speeches live.

Opposite top: The first Buckingham Palace Company of Girl Guides numbers among its members Princess Elizabeth and Princess Margaret. The company is made up of girls from all walks of life and first aid is one of the leading subjects practised. Princess Elizabeth is seen here tying a sling on a 'patient'

Opposite bottom: Harvest time at Sandringham. The Royal Princess has a word with one of the farm workers.

Opposite: Princess Elizabeth married Lieutenant Philip Mountbatten in a glittering ceremony on 20th November 1947. Earlier that day he had been given the title Prince Philip, Duke of Edinburgh by the King. Her dress was designed by Norman Hartnell. After a simple ceremony, the wedding breakfast was held at Buckingham Palace where the five-hundred-pound wedding cake was cut using the sword of the bridegroom's grandfather. Afterwards they drove to Waterloo Station to honeymoon at Broadlands in Hampshire. They were to live at Clarence House. The following year Princess Elizabeth gave birth to their first son, Charles Philip Arthur George on 14th November.

Above: Elizabeth attended a dinner given at the French Embassy with her parents in March 1950.

Right: In October 1950 the Princess arrives at the Royal College of Music in London to fulfil her first public engagement since the birth of Princess Anne in August.

Relaxing at Balmoral

Opposite: The Royal Princesses play with Princess Anne in the grounds of Balmoral Castle in August 1951. It was the day after Princess Margaret's twenty first birthday.

Right: Princess Elizabeth and Princess Margaret leave Westminster Hall together after the State Opening of Parliament.

Below: An opportunity for Princess Elizabeth and the Duke of Edinburgh to spend time with Prince Charles and Princess Anne in the grounds of Clarence House – their London home at the time. They were due to sail from Liverpool for Quebec on 25th September 1951 in the Canadian Pacific liner 'Empress of France' to begin a tour of Canada.

It was evident that year that her father's health was beginning to fail and in February, Princess Elizabeth stood in for him at the traditional Trooping of the Colour ceremony. He was however, able to inaugurate the Festival of Britain in May and open the Royal Festival Hall on the South Bank. Later in the year, lung disease was diagnosed and his left lung removed.

Her Majesty The Queen

The Queen's father, George VI, passed away in his sleep on 6th February 1952 and the nation mourned the passing of a popular King. The Coronation was planned for the following year on 2nd June 1953.

Right: Elizabeth made her first official Christmas Day broadcast as monarch to the United Kingdom and throughout the world. It was recorded live at Sandringham House in Norfolk in 1952. Later in 1957 she decided to switch to the medium of television for all future broadcasts.

Below: King Feisal and the Regent of Iraq joined Queen Elizabeth, the Duke of Edinburgh and Princess Anne in the grounds of Balmoral Castle in September 1952.

Opposite: The Queen begins her journey from the Palace to Westminster Abbey for her coronation. Her gown was encrusted with golden crystals and pearls. She wore an ermine cape and diamond tiara, earrings and necklace.

The Coronation was a carefully planned state occasion, which was celebrated all around the country. As everyone looked to the future it seemed fitting that on the morning of the Coronation it was announced that Everest had been conquered for the first time.

The Queen's arrival at Westminster Abbey

Opposite: The Queen travelled to her coronation in the gold state coach. It was a magnificent occasion, which showed British pageantry at its best. More than ten thousand servicemen and two thousand bandsmen followed the coach. On arrival at the Abbey, she pauses while the footmen and Maids of Honour arrange the magnificent silk train.

Above: The Queen sits in the St. Edward's chair in a simple white dress. She prepares for the solemn ceremony of the Anointing. Four Knights of the Garter prepare to hold the Canopy above her Majesty.

The Coronation of Queen Elizabeth II

The climax of the Coronation Ceremony arrives. Dr Fisher, the Archbishop of Canterbury places the Crown on the head of Her Majesty. In her left hand she holds the Rod with Dove, which signifies equity and mercy. In her right is the Sceptre with cross, which signifies kingly power and justice. She was crowned with the St Edward's Crown but later exchanged it for the lighter Imperial State Crown for the journey back to the Palace.

Opposite: The Queen takes the Chair of Estate after making her humble adoration and saying private prayers. She is just beneath the Royal Gallery.

Royal Air Force salutes the crowned Queen

After the ceremony a formal procession took the family back to Buckingham Palace. In the evening they appeared on the balcony to wave to the vast cheering crowd below and to watch the Royal Air Force flypast salute. Prince Charles and Princess Anne were fascinated by the proceedings.

Derby parade

Below: The Queen and Queen Mother at the Derby Parade in June 1954. Winner of the Derby Stakes that year was Lester Piggott riding Never Say Die (an outsider at 33-1!).

Right: In December 1953, the Queen made a Christmas broadcast to the peoples of the British Commonwealth from Government House, Auckland, New Zealand.

Opposite: The Queen was photographed in 1954 leaving Hutchinson House after the wedding reception of her friend and Coronation Maid of Honour, Lady Mary Baillie-Hamilton, to Mr Adrian Bailey.

Balmoral 1955

Opposite: During the annual family holiday at Balmoral in August 1955 the Queen spent time with Princess Anne playing with their pony called Greensleeves. Balmoral Castle is the private property of the sovereign located on Deeside in West Aberdeenshire. It was a favourite residence of Queen Victoria and had been purchased by Prince Albert in 1852. The castle was then rebuilt three years later. Queen Victoria often held court there and since then the Royal Family has kept up the annual custom of staying there during the shooting season.

Above: Elizabeth arrived at Victoria Palace for the annual Royal Variety Show in November 1955.

Left: Swathed in white mink the Queen attended the Order of the Bath ceremony in Westminster Abbey in November 1956.

Queen presents the prizes

Above left: In 1957 the Horse of the Year Show was held in Harringay. The Queen was there to present the Jorrocks Cup (for the leading show jumper of the year) to Ted Williams for the third year in succession.

Opposite: 28th May 1957. The Queen arrived to watch the Household Brigade Polo match in which the Duke of Edinburgh was playing at Windsor Great Park. She was accompanied by one of her pet corgis.

Above: Smiling to the crowds, the Queen left St. Bride's Church in Fleet Street after a re-dedication service in December 1957. The church had been restored after excessive damage in the air raids during the Second World War.

Left: The Queen attended the premiere of 'Dunkirk' with Lord Mountbatten in March 1958. He was apparently responsible for introducing the guests to the Queen but after introducing several guests by the wrong the name, Elizabeth calmly took control of the situation and greeted people herself!

Bicentenary at Kew

Opposite: In June 1959 the Queen and Prince Philip attended a garden party at Kew to celebrate the bicentenary of the Royal Botanic Gardens. She visited the renovated Palm House, which had been re-opened after seven years and joined her guests for tea in the Orangery. It was two hundred years since the gardens had been taken over by Princess Augusta, mother of George III.

Below: In November 1958 the Vice-President of the United States of America, Richard Nixon and his wife were on an official four-day visit to England. They held a dinner at the American Embassy in honour of Her Majesty.

Right: Another premiere later in 1958 when the Queen and Prince Philip attended the new Danny Kaye film 'Me and the Colonel' at the Odeon, Leicester Square. Nicole Maurey curtsies to the Queen and alongside are Mr and Mrs Kurt Jurgens.

Windsor Castle 1959

Quiet moments for the Queen and Prince Philip at Windsor Castle in 1959. Sugar the Queen's corgi accompanied them throughout the photo call. In June, the Queen began an extensive tour of Canada and the United States. She had just discovered that she was pregnant again, but carried on, determined to carry out her plans. A romance had begun between Princess Margaret and Antony Armstrong-Jones, which was to lead to their marriage the following year.

Thirty-fifth birthday

Opposite top right: The Queen was seen on her thirty-fifth birthday in April 1961 with the Duke of Beaufort at Badminton House. She was attending the three-day horse trials with other members of the Royal Family.

Opposite left: John F. Kennedy and his wife dined with the Queen at Buckingham Palace in June 1961. They were in London for a whirlwind visit and returned to America the next day.

Opposite below right: The Queen presented the John Player trophy to Britain's Pat Smythe in July 1961. The International Horse Show Jumping Competition took place at the White City Stadium in London.

Left: Winner of the men's singles at Wimbledon in 1962 was Australian Rod Laver.

Below: The Queen shakes hands with Cliff Richard in the foyer at the London Palladium after the Royal Command Performance on October 29th 1962. To his left is Rosemary Clooney and to his right, Harry Secombe and Eartha Kitt.

Brother for four-year-old Andrew

Opposite: In 1963 the Queen toured Australia. While in Sydney she made an unscheduled stop at Moore Park, a children's playground. She obviously enjoyed the informality of the occasion watching the antics of the children and some of their pets.

Right: This was the first official photograph (taken by Cecil Beaton) of the Queen with her fourth child Prince Edward, clutching the finger of his four-year-old brother Andrew. He was born on 10th March 1964. The crib was used by the Queen and Princess Margaret and all the Queen's children.

Below: The Queen allowed her family to be photographed in the grounds of Frogmore, Windsor for the occasion of her thirty-ninth birthday. Frogmore House is a former Royal Home in Home Park below Windsor Castle. It was believed to be a favourite of Queen Victoria in her long widowhood.

Frogmore, Windsor

Opposite: In the grounds of Frogmore, Windsor.

In February the Queen, after careful thought, had visited her uncle, the Duke of Windsor, for the first time in twenty-nine years. He was at a London clinic having an eye operation. He asked if he and the Duchess could be buried in the family burial ground at Frogmore, Windsor when they died. The Queen granted this wish.

Left: The Queen and Duke of Edinburgh attended the Gala performance of 'Tosca' at Covent Garden in July 1965. She is seen with the Earl of Drogheda.

Below: In July 1965, the Queen carried out the first official visit to the Isle of Wight by a reigning monarch since 1671. At Carisbrooke Castle she installed Earl Mountbatten as 'Governor and Captain of all our Isle of Wight'.

In 1966 the Queen reached the age of forty and Prince Charles celebrated his eighteenth birthday. This meant that he could replace his father as the possible Regent if the Queen was ever incapacitated. One of the most enjoyable duties she carried out that year was to present the World Cup to Bobby Moore and the England team after they beat West Germany 4-2!

Royal Variety

Below: At the Royal Variety Performance at the London Palladium in 1965, the Queen was introduced to the Liverpool comedian Ken Dodd. Also presented were Max Bygraves, Spike Milligan and Dudley Moore.

Right: November 1966. The Queen attended the St. Cecilia Festival Royal Concert at the Royal Albert Hall in aid of music profession charities.

Opposite: A family gathering for the Queen's 42nd birthday (1968) in the gardens at Frogmore, Windsor. Charles, aged 19, Anne 17, Andrew 8 and Edward 4.

Prince Charles was at university studying archaeology and anthropology (he later changed to history). Princess Anne was at Benenden and about to take two 'A' levels. Both were now more involved with public and state occasions. Prince Andrew and Prince Edward were still kept out of the public eye.

Going underground

Opposite bottom: The new Victoria Line was officially opened by the Queen in March 1969. The journey was the first a reigning monarch had ever made by underground. The line stretched from Victoria to Walthamstow and was the first in-town underground to be built for more than sixty years. New features included closed circuit television for passengers, automatic trains and fare collection.

Above: After the premiere of 'Doctor Dolittle' at the Odeon, Leicester Square. Joan Collins and William Dix were introduced to the Queen.

Right: In December 1968 the Queen attended a dedication service in St George's Chapel, Windsor and was met by the Very Reverend John Woods, Dean of Windsor. She was presented with two silver candlesticks each measuring four foot six inches high. They were presented by the Royal Air Force to mark its fiftieth anniversary. They were to stand on the altar in the nave in the chapel. Princess Anne accompanied her.

Opposite top: The President of the United States, Richard Nixon, joined the Queen and the Duke of Edinburgh for lunch at Buckingham Palace in February 1969.

Coming of age

Left: May 1969 saw the twentieth anniversary ceremony of Signature of Statute of Council of Europe at the Banqueting Hall in Whitehall. The Royal couple were greeted by the Prime Minister, Harold Wilson.

Below: In 1969, a series of photographs was specially taken to show the informal life of Prince Charles, who was to be invested as Prince of Wales on 1st July. At the time Prince Edward was five years old.

Opposite top: Prince Charles accompanied his grandmother as they walked back to Sandringham after a church service.

Opposite below: Prince Charles attended the Army Benevolent Fund's twenty-fifth anniversary Variety Performance, 'Fall in the Stars'. His parents and sister, Princess Anne, accompanied him.

Investiture of
The Prince of Wales

Above: A major Royal occasion as the Investiture takes place at Caernarvon Castle. The Investiture was initially overshadowed by threats of violence from the Welsh nationalists. Despite this, the Prince spent eight weeks at the University of Wales learning some of the language, culture and history of the Principality. It was a spectacular occasion with great pageantry. The ceremony had changed very little since Edward III invested the Black Prince in 1343. Most of the design was created by the Earl of Snowdon in his role as Constable of Caernarvon.

Left: Princess Anne celebrated her twenty-first birthday at Thurso. She had just come ashore from the Royal Yacht Britannia. Later that day, the family drove to the Queen Mother's holiday home, the Castle of May.

Opposite top: Christmas Day 1971 saw the Royal Family leave St. George's Chapel at Windsor Castle after attending morning service.

Opposite below: The Treasures of Tutankhamun was a major exhibition in London in 1972. The general public queued for many hours to see the treasures. The Queen attended and is seen studying the famous 'Golden Mask'.

Silver wedding anniversary

Above and opposite below: The Queen and Duke of Edinburgh's silver wedding anniversary took place in 1972. They allowed a series of photographs to be taken to honour the event, these were taken at Balmoral Castle.

Opposite top: In June 1972 the Queen visited St. Peter's Church of England School in Ebury Street, London. She joined them to mark the school's centenary celebrations.

Joining with Europe

Above: Britain joined the Common Market in 1972 and in January 1973 the Queen attended a gala launching 'Fanfare for Europe', the official festival that marked Britain's entry. Joined by the Prime Minister Edward Heath, she attended the event at the Royal Opera House, Covent Garden.

Right: Visiting the Headquarters of the Boys and Girls Brigade at Parsons Green, London in February 1973.

Opposite top: A very sombre and private moment for the Queen after she laid a wreath on the huge slate cross in the village cemetery of Aberfan, Wales. In 1966 one hundred and sixteen children and twenty-eight adults had lost their lives when the tip collapsed on the local school. She afterwards opened a new community centre and said 'I have been most impressed by what has been achieved in this community – now happily no longer under the shadow of the huge tips which have been taken away from the hillside'.

Opposite below: Thousands watched the Queen arrive for the premiere of 'Lost Horizon' at the Odeon in Leicester Square in March 1973. The film starred Peter Finch, Sally Kellerman and Sir John Gielgud. Eric Morecambe and Ernie Wise soon reduced her to helpless laughter!

Badminton horse trials

Above: Determined to get a good view, the Queen and other members of the Royal Family perched on an improvised hay-cart to view the cross-country event at the Badminton horse trials in April 1973. An aerial was fixed to the cart to enable them to view a television. Left to right: Lord Linley; Lady Sarah Armstrong Jones; the Duke of Beaufort; the Earl of Snowdon and the Queen Mother.

Opposite: The party also had the opportunity to look at the hounds belonging to the Duke of Beaufort.

Birthday salute!

Above and right: The Queen celebrated her forty-eighth birthday at Windsor in 1974. She took the salute and reviewed the Queen's Scouts. Afterwards she met a party of twelve handicapped scouts.

In February that year, the Queen was in Indonesia when she learned that Princess Anne had just survived a kidnap attempt as she and Mark Phillips were being driven down the Mall. A gunman tried to force her out of the car and in the frenzy that followed the incident, four people were shot and wounded. A review of security was immediately ordered by the Prime Minister, Harold Wilson.

Opposite: At the Royal Windsor Horse Show in May 1974, Prince Charles accompanied the Queen with his current girlfriend, the Countess of Westmorland. The Duke of Edinburgh was competing in the marathon section of the Barclay's Bank International Driving Grand Prix.

The Queen's bodyguard

July 1974. Her Majesty inspected the Queen's bodyguard of the Yeoman of the Guard at Buckingham Palace.

Opposite top: The Queen was joined at The Royal Windsor Horse Show by King Constantine of Greece (left) and Mr John Ambler, husband of Princess Margarethe of Sweden.

Opposite bottom: The Queen at the Chelsea Flower Show.

Charles's birthday treat

Opposite: On Prince Charles's twenty-sixth birthday, he accompanied the Queen and Princess Alexandra to a performance of Alan Ayckbourn's play 'Third Person Singular' at the Vaudeville Theatre.

Above left: Introductions were made to the England cricket team just before the second Test against Australia in July 1975. Captain Tony Greig (just behind the Queen) introduces Dennis Amiss.

Above right: The Queen attended the premiere of 'Rooster Cogburn' in December 1975 at the Odeon, Leicester Square. The premiere was in aid of the Police Dependents Trust. A bouquet was presented by Laura Gisbourne, aged 9, the daughter of Police Inspector David Gisbourne. He had died the previous year in the Red Lion riots.

Right: Crowds greeted her at the top of Butser Hill when she officially opened the new Queen Elizabeth Country Park, near Petersfield in August 1976. It is one of the largest in Britain and includes 540 acres of open downland and 860 acres in the adjoining Queen Elizabeth Forest.

Silver Jubilee

In 1977 the whole country celebrated the Silver Jubilee. Crowds in London lined the route to watch the Jubilee celebrations. Afterwards H.M Queen and Prince Philip waved from the balcony at Buckingham Palace.

Opposite: Prince Edward was her companion at the Badminton Horse Trials in April 1976.

The country rejoices

The official week of festivities for the Silver Jubilee in June 1977 began with the Queen lighting a giant bonfire in Windsor Great Park. It was the first of a hundred beacons all around the country that lit the skies. Everywhere people celebrated holding street parties and when she attended the thanksgiving service at St. Paul's, over a million people lined the procession route. Wherever she went she was met with enthusiasm and great warmth. To mark the anniversary, she undertook an extensive tour of the world.

Right and below: On 7th June the family attended a thanksgiving service at St. Paul's Cathedral.

Opposite top: In 1978 the Queen and Prince Philip undertook a four day visit to the Channel Islands. On a walkabout at St Peter Port in Guernsey she was swamped by flowers from the crowds who lined the narrow streets.

Opposite below: Walking through The Lanes in Brighton The Queen is again deluged with flowers. One young girl presented a tiny Lily of the Valley flower posy.

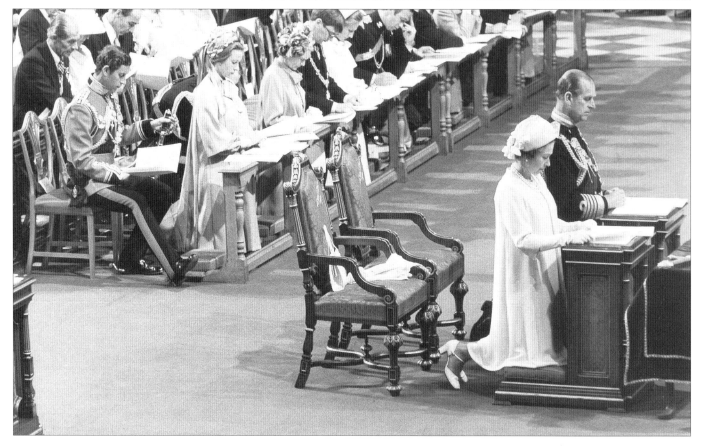

Balmoral 1979

Right, below and opposite: The Queen and Duke of Edinburgh's thirty-second wedding anniversary in 1979. The family were photographed at Balmoral Castle.

1979 began with a three-week tour of the Gulf. It was the first time she had visited these oil-rich countries and she was showered with luxury wherever she went. In Saudi Arabia she was designated an 'honorary gentleman' to overcome the strict rules women had to follow.

On 27th August the Royal Family were devastated by the news that Lord Mountbatten had been assassinated by the IRA. A major influence on the family, he was especially close to Prince Charles as a friend and mentor. His funeral service took place at Westminster Abbey.

Charles marries

Opposite: After announcing their engagement in February, Prince Charles married Lady Diana Spencer on 29th July 1981. The wedding took place at St. Paul's Cathedral. A formal acknowledgement to the monarch was an essential part of the service led by the Archbishop of Canterbury.

Above: After the service and the procession back to Buckingham Palace, the family gathered on the balcony.

The press had been speculating for years as to when Prince Charles would marry. The wedding was an amazing spectacle, which was watched by hundreds of millions around the world. Afterwards the couple honeymooned on the Royal Yacht Britannia before joining the rest of the family at Balmoral. Eleven months later, their first child Prince William was born. He was second in line to the throne.

Right: Later in 1981 the Queen and Prince Philip left Heathrow with Prince Edward to fly to Balmoral for the start of their annual holiday.

At the Highland Games

Above: During the holiday the Royal Family attended the Braemar Highland Games. The Prince and Princess of Wales made their first public appearance since their wedding.

Right: The Queen officially opened the modernised headquarters of the Royal British Legion in Pall Mall, London in November 1981.

Opposite top: Only two days later the Queen was in Birmingham on her thirty-fourth wedding anniversary. She enjoyed a joke with schoolgirls while on walkabout in Chamberlain Square.

Opposite below: The Queen and Princess Anne in May 1983 on their way to Horse Guards Parade.

Centenary walkabout

Opposite and right: The Queen officially opened the gardens surrounding Croydon Town Hall in June 1983 to mark the centenary of Croydon's municipal charter.

Below: The Queen and Prince Philip arrived at Newmarket for the Annual Stallion Show of the National Light Horse Breeding Society in March 1984.

In the same month the Queen and Prince Philip paid a four-day visit to Jordan amidst very tight security. Their host King Hussein had recently escaped an assassination attempt.

On 15th September Prince Harry was born to the Prince and Princess of Wales – the Queen's fourth grandchild. He was christened Henry Charles Albert David.

Heads of State

Opposite below: In June 1984, the Queen hosted a special banquet at Buckingham Palace to follow the London Economic Summit. Among the guests were the US President Ronald Reagan and British Premier Margaret Thatcher.

Above: Heads of State attending the banquet: (left to right) Chancellor Helmut Kohl of West Germany, Ronald Reagan, Margaret Thatcher, Prime Minister Yasuhiro Nakasone of Japan and President Francois Mitterrand of France.

Opposite top: At the Annual Stallion Show.

Official residence

December 1985. The Queen attended a celebration dinner at 10 Downing Street to mark the 250th anniversary of the use of number 10 as the official residence of the Prime Minister. During that time the house had been occupied by forty-eight different Prime Ministers. Pictured with the Queen are the six most recent. Left to right: James Callaghan, Lord Home, Margaret Thatcher, Lord Stockton, Harold Wilson and Edward Heath.

Hampton Court

March 1986. The Queen visited Hampton Court Palace to look at the fire damaged south wing. She continued to visit to watch the progress of the restoration work.

Opposite top: The Queen was pictured with the Princess of Wales and her nephew Lord Linley outside Clarence House. It was the Queen Mother's eighty-seventh birthday and after greeting well-wishers, the family joined her for lunch.

Maundy services

Opposite top right: Accompanied by the Lord Bishop of Lichfield, the Right Reverend Keith Sutton, the Queen attended the Maundy Service at Lichfield Cathedral in March 1988. During the Service, she distributed the Royal Maundy Money to sixty-two men and sixty-two women, all from the Diocese of Lichfield and all over sixty-five years of age. The Queen has attended 46 Royal Maundy services in 35 cathedrals during her reign. A total of 5,100 people have received Maundy Money in recognition of their service to the Church and their communities.

Opposite below: After the service she greeted the waiting crowds with the Duke of Edinburgh.

Opposite top left: The Queen plants the replacement for the unique Tilia Petiolaris 'Chelsea Sentinel' in the grounds of the Royal Hospital, Chelsea.

Above: March 1989 saw the Queen perform the Maundy Service at St. Philip's Cathedral in Birmingham. During the walkabout afterwards, one of the waiting crowd reduced her to helpless laughter when they read out the contents of an Easter card!

Greetings from the Royal Family

The Princess of Wales and Princess Margaret were among the members of the Royal Family who joined the Queen to greet Nigeria's President, General Ibrahim Babangida and his wife Maryam at Victoria Station. They were on a three-day visit to Britain.

Opposite top: The Queen and Princess Margaret had the opportunity to go backstage at the Royal Opera House in December 1991. Earlier they had watched a rehearsal of the Royal Ballet's Christmas Show 'The Nutcracker'.

Opposite below: In 1993 the Queen and Princess Margaret, along with other members of the family, joined the Queen Mother to celebrate her ninety -third birthday at Clarence House.

D-Day remembered

A quiet moment for the monarch as she walked through the gravestones at Bayeux cemetery after a D-Day commemoration service.

Opposite: The Queen reads the annual speech at the State Opening of Parliament in November 1995.
She announces on behalf of the Government the agenda for political and legislative affairs for the coming year.

Royal website online

The Queen visited Kingsbury High School, Brent to celebrate the launch of the Royal website in March 1997. Pupil Christopher Bailey demonstrated the program on screen.

In August 1997, Diana, Princess of Wales was killed in a car crash in Paris. Although now separated from Prince Charles, her untimely death stunned the nation. The area in front of Kensington Palace, her London home, became a shrine as people flocked to pay their last respects. Known as the 'People's Princess', the whole country came to a standstill when her funeral was held at Westminster Abbey on Saturday 6th September.

Left: April 1998 saw the first rock band to perform at Buckingham Palace. The concert was held after an official dinner for the Asia-European leaders. She met with the vocalist Julie Thompson.

Opposite: The Queen and the Duke of Edinburgh attended the Garter Ceremony in Windsor in June 1999.

Edward marries

Opposite top: Accompanied by his brothers Prince Charles and Prince Andrew, Prince Edward walked through the grounds of Windsor Castle to St. George's Chapel where he was to marry Sophie Rhys-Jones in June 1999.

Opposite below: The Queen met Pope John Paul II for talks at the Vatican in October 2000. Accompanied by Prince Philip she was dressed in black velvet with a black veil as is the Vatican tradition for visiting female heads of state.

Above: The Queen was accompanied by Barbara Windsor during a visit to Elstree Studios in November 2001, as they walked through the sets of Albert Square and the Queen Vic.

Chippenham walkabout

The Queen made a visit to Chippenham, Wiltshire in December 2001. After travelling there by train she spent the day meeting well-wishers and visited the Dyson factory.

Opposite: The Queen with her aunt Princess Alice.

Looking to the future: The Golden Jubilee 2002

Opposite: Recording the traditional Christmas broadcast to the Commonwealth in December 2001.

Above: After attending the Christmas Day service in 2001 at the Church of St. Mary Magdalen on the Sandringham Estate, Norfolk, the Queen is once again deluged with flowers from the waiting crowds.

The Queen is the fifth longest serving British monarch. She becomes the fourth longest serving monarch on 21 June 2002. Only four other kings and queens in British history have reigned for 50 years or more: Victoria (63 years); George III (59 years); Henry III (56 years); Edward III (50 years). In 50 remarkable years, the Queen has undertaken 251 official overseas visits to 128 different countries. By the end of 2002, the Queen will have visited Australia 14 times, Canada 20 times, Jamaica 6 times and New Zealand 10 times.

Additional picture credits
1; 2; 3; 8; 18T; 28T & B; 29; 32; 33TR & TL; 40; 41T;
50T; 56; 59; 64; 70; 71T; 78; 79; 80; 81; 85T & B; 86; 87;
88T & B; 89; 90T & B; 91; 92; 93; 95.
Copyright Press Association photographs:
Front Cover copyright CPNA